Cambridge Discovery Education™
▶ INTERACTIVE READERS

Series editor: Bob Hastings

POISON
MEDICINE, MURDER, AND MYSTERY

B2+

Caroline Shackleton and Nathan Paul Turner

CAMBRIDGE
UNIVERSITY PRESS

Discovery
EDUCATION™

CAMBRIDGE
UNIVERSITY PRESS

32 Avenue of the Americas, New York, NY 10013-2473, USA

Cambridge University Press is part of the University of Cambridge.

It furthers the University's mission by disseminating knowledge in the pursuit of
education, learning and research at the highest international levels of excellence.

www.cambridge.org
Information on this title: www.cambridge.org/9781107622609

© Cambridge University Press 2014

First published 2014
3rd printing 2015

Printed in Hong Kong, China, by Golden Cup Printing Company Limited

A catalogue record for this publication is available from the British Library

Library of Congress Cataloging in Publication Data

Shackleton, Caroline.
    Poison : medicine, murder, and mystery / Caroline Shackleton and Nathan Paul Turner.
       pages cm. — (Cambridge discovery interactive readers)
    ISBN 978-1-107-62260-9 (pbk. : alk. paper)
 1. Poisons—Juvenile literature. 2. English language—Textbooks for foreign speakers.
 3. Readers (Elementary) I. Title.

RA1214.S52 2013
615.9'05—dc23

                                    2013016511

ISBN 978-1-107-62260-9

Additional resources for this publication at www.cambridge.org

Layout services, art direction, book design, and photo research: Q2ABillSMITH GROUP
Editorial services: Hyphen S.A.
Audio production: CityVox, New York
Video production: Q2ABillSMITH GROUP

Contents

Before You Read: Get Ready!

Poison, any chemical mixture that causes a breakdown in an animal's normal bodily functions, can cause sickness or even death. Where do poisons come from and how are they used?

Words to Know

Complete the sentences with the correct words.

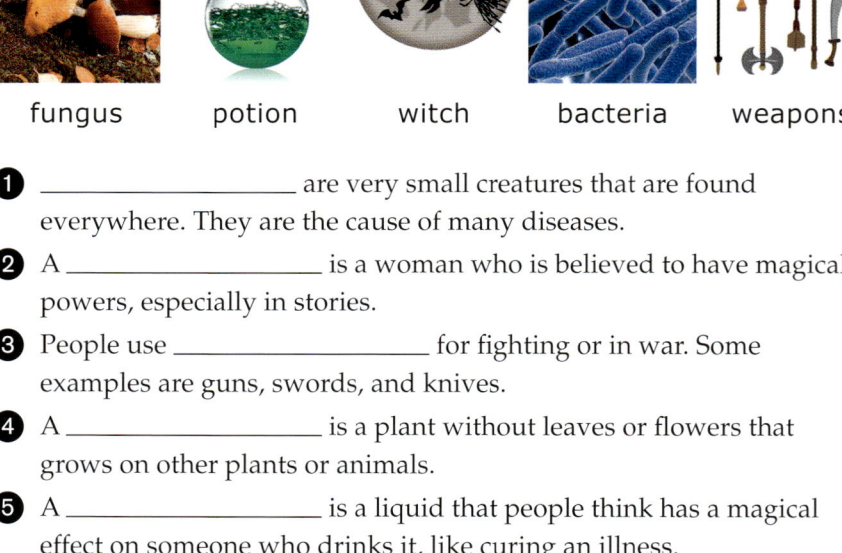

fungus   potion   witch   bacteria   weapons

❶ _____ are very small creatures that are found everywhere. They are the cause of many diseases.

❷ A _____ is a woman who is believed to have magical powers, especially in stories.

❸ People use _____ for fighting or in war. Some examples are guns, swords, and knives.

❹ A _____ is a plant without leaves or flowers that grows on other plants or animals.

❺ A _____ is a liquid that people think has a magical effect on someone who drinks it, like curing an illness.

Words to Know

Read the paragraph. Then complete the definitions with the correct <mark>highlighted</mark> words.

Poisons have been used for thousands of years. At first, poisons were used for hunting animals: large <mark>prey</mark> could be killed more easily with their help. Later, poisons were also used in war. The illegal use of poisons to make people ill or kill them also goes back a very long time. People have had many different <mark>motives</mark> for using poison to kill people. Often, it was to reach a position of power, or to remove somebody in order to get the money from their <mark>inheritance</mark>. When banks started selling life <mark>insurance</mark>, people used poison on their family members simply to claim the money! This became very common in the 19th century, when a powerful poison, <mark>arsenic</mark>, was commonly used. Nowadays, doctors have many <mark>antidotes</mark> to poisons, and can often save the <mark>victim</mark> if called in time.

1 _____ : money, property, or possessions you can get from someone after the person has died

2 _____ : the agreement in which you pay a company money, and the company pays the cost if you have an accident, injury, or loss

3 _____ : a strong poison that is often used to kill rats and can kill people

4 _____ : a creature that is hunted and killed for food by another animal

5 _____ : chemicals that act against the bad effects of a poison to limit the harm it can do

6 _____ : a person who has suffered the effects of violence, illness, or bad luck

7 _____ : strong reasons for doing something

? PREDICT
Where do poisons come from? Make a list of possible sources and check your list as you read.

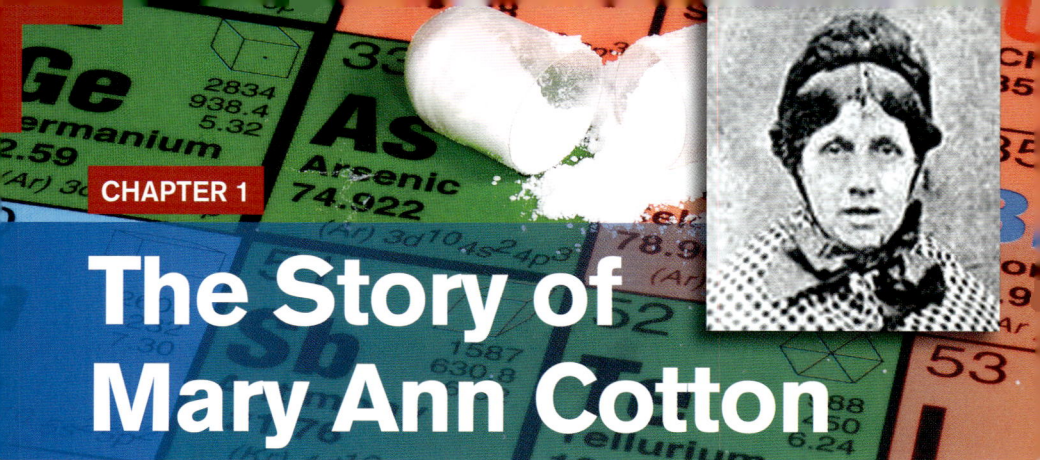

CHAPTER 1

The Story of Mary Ann Cotton

COLD, CRUEL, AND PAINFUL, MURDER BY POISON HAS BEEN SEEN THROUGHOUT HISTORY AS A TRULY HORRIBLE CRIME. MORE HORRIBLE YET, IN MARY ANN COTTON'S CASE THE VICTIMS WERE MEMBERS OF HER OWN FAMILY.

The background

Mary Ann Cotton, a nurse, was born in the north of England in 1832 to a very religious family. In spite of her hard upbringing, Mary was described as a kind and open girl.

Victims

It is thought that in total Mary Cotton killed 21 people, including her mother, three of her four husbands, a lover, and twelve children.

Mary's motives

The main reason seems to have been money. All but one of her husbands had taken out insurance policies, and Mary received large payments upon their deaths.

How she kept it all secret

In those days, the average rate of death was much higher in England, especially among children, so no one thought the deaths were strange. Also, communication was slow, and Mary moved around to avoid suspicion.

How she did it

All of Mary's **victims** apparently died from stomach illnesses, but in fact this condition has very similar symptoms to the deadly poison arsenic. In the 19th century, arsenic was freely available and was often used as a cleaning product.

A lucky escape

Her third husband James Robinson became suspicious when, after the deaths of their children, she tried to convince him to get life insurance. He threw her out and saved his own life.

Brought to justice

Eventually, Mary's strange behavior and the death of her fourth husband's son caused suspicion, and the case was investigated. The dead boy was found to have huge quantities of arsenic in his stomach. In 1873 Mary was arrested, put on trial, found guilty of murder, and hanged. Even at the end, she continued to say she was innocent.

?

EVALUATE

Do you think Mary Ann Cotton could get away with these crimes today? Why or why not?

CHAPTER 2

The Nature of Poison

WHAT IS A POISON AND HOW DOES IT WORK? TAKE A LOOK AT SOME FASCINATING – AND DEADLY – CHEMICAL MIXTURES.

Some creatures sting their victims.

A poison can be thought of as any chemical **substance** that causes a harmful change in the body. Medically, it is hard to define a poison, because any substance introduced in large enough quantities can cause illness, harm bodily **functions**, or cause death. This difficulty has been understood since ancient times, and the Ancient Greeks even used the same word, *pharmakon*, for both medicines and poisons.

A poison that exists naturally in an insect or animal, and which is often introduced into the victim by biting or stinging, is known as a venom, while one in a plant is generally known as a toxin. Until the advance of the science of chemistry in the 19th century, most poisons used by humans were either venoms or toxins.

Plant poisons

Plants cannot move to escape the animals that feed on them, so they have other ways to protect themselves. Many have become **toxic** as a means of defense. Plant toxins range from those that simply bother the skin to those that cause pain or death when eaten.

It is surprising just how many common plants, flowers, and fruits are poisonous. Even fruits that we eat on a daily basis, such as apples, have seeds[1] that contain deadly poisons, though in very small amounts. Interestingly, many plants are also toxic to other plants, so certain plants should not be placed together in a garden.

Traditionally, plants have been used as medicines to help people and as poisons to kill them. Some plants can be used as both. The plant wolfsbane, for example, was used as a weapon to poison water and arrows, but was also highly valued by doctors for treating the flu and high blood pressure.

....
[1]**seed:** a small part of a plant from which a new plant can grow

Wolfsbane was used as a weapon and a medicine.

Insects

The use of venoms is very common in the insect world, and most people are familiar with the venomous sting of bees or wasps. To people, both stings are painful, but these venoms serve different purposes. Bee venom is used for defense and is designed to cause

A wasp's sting immobilizes its prey.

pain; wasp venom is used to **immobilize** prey.

Frogs

There are many types of poisonous frogs. Most produce their venom through their skin and are poisonous to eat or to touch. Many South American tribes have traditionally used the venom of the poison dart frog on their arrows when hunting. Some types of poison dart frog venom contain enough poison to kill ten adult humans. Scientists believe that these frogs do not actually produce their own venom, but take it from ants and other insects that they eat.

Poison dart frogs have poisonous skin.

Snakes

When people talk of poisons, the one animal that usually comes to mind is the snake. Snakes have been feared and admired for thousands of years for their terrible venoms. The venom is usually introduced into the victim through little tubes in the snake's teeth, or fangs, and is mostly used to immobilize the prey.

Vipers use their fangs to deliver venom.

Many snakes have enough venom to kill an adult human easily. Fortunately, snakes are naturally shy and try to stay away from people. But every year tens of thousands of people, as well as many more farm animals, die from snakebites.

This has led to serious interest in producing antidotes to snakebites. One antidote against snake venom is to use the venom itself in small amounts to help the body's defense system "learn" about it. The body gradually learns to defend itself.

Video Quest

Viper milking

Watch this video about viper milking. Where are vipers found? Why are vipers milked?

CHAPTER 3

The History of Poison

HUMANS HAVE PROVED TO BE VERY QUICK LEARNERS! POISONS HAVE BEEN USED IN ALL SORTS OF DEADLY WAYS.

The first poisons

The earliest evidence for the use of poison goes back more than 4,500 years. It was originally used for hunting and in war. There are many ancient descriptions of poisoned spears and arrows. In fact, our modern word *toxic* originally came from the Ancient Greek word for "poison arrow." Poison was not limited to weapons, however. The ancient Assyrians used to poison their enemies' water supplies using ergot, a toxic substance that grows on plants.

As knowledge of poisons grew, they started to be used in peacetime too, for example as punishment. The Athenians considered poison a kinder way to die and sometimes used it when executing people. When the philosopher Socrates was sentenced to death, he was allowed to drink the poison hemlock in the company of his friends.

Poisons were also used to get rid of unwanted competitors. By the first century BCE, many rulers employed official tasters, usually slaves, to taste all their food and drink. The famous Greek King of Pontus, Mithridates, even went on a search for the perfect antidote to all poisons. Although it is doubtful that his **potion**, *Mithridatium*, was effective, it became extremely popular.

Ancient Rome

The Latin word for poison, *venenum*, is related to Venus, the goddess of love, and originally meant a "love potion." Funnily enough, the first recorded use of poison in Rome was in 331 BCE, when a large group of women were convicted of helping each other to murder their husbands! Poison later became such a problem in Rome that a special law was created against it. The law had little effect, however, and poisoners continued their deadly business.

Venus, goddess of love

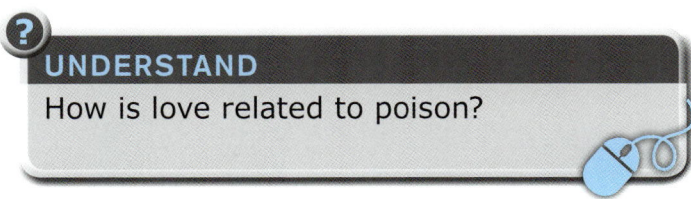

?

UNDERSTAND

How is love related to poison?

Some poisoners of the time, like Locusta, became extremely wealthy. This infamous[2] lady murdered many people – including Emperor[3] Claudius – at the orders of his wife, Agrippina. A year later, after poisoning another victim, she was arrested and sentenced to death.

Emperor Nero, however, saved Locusta from execution and gave her wealth, land, and slaves. She became Nero's private poisoner, practicing her mixtures on slaves and murdering Nero's enemies. But Locusta's luck changed when Nero died. Without her protector, she was again sentenced to death for her crimes. She was not poisoned, however; she was torn to pieces by wild animals!

The Middle Ages

By the 8th century CE, Arabian doctors had found ways to produce arsenic so that it was clear and had little smell, making it almost unnoticeable and very popular. In fact, arsenic became so widely used among the rich and powerful, as a convenient way to deal with opponents, that it eventually became known as "inheritance powder."

In both medieval France and Italy, rich and important families were constantly fighting over inheritances, land, and power.

[2]**infamous:** famous for being bad
[3]**emperor:** a male ruler of a group of countries

Some of the most feared poisoners of the day belonged to the infamous Borgia family.

Originally from an important Spanish family, Rodrigo Borgia became head of the Roman Catholic Church in 1492, through a combination of family favors and bribery.[4] Once in Rome, he placed his own children in positions of power and attempted to conquer Italy.

The Borgias were well-known for poisoning important members of the Catholic Church and taking their wealth. Rodrigo himself, some say, was actually the mistaken victim of one of his own poisons.

There was even a rumor that Borgia's daughter, Lucrezia, kept a specially sweetened type of arsenic hidden in a ring. With her back turned, she opened the ring and secretly poured the arsenic into her victims' drinks.

People said that Lucrezia Borgia kept arsenic in a special ring.

[4]**bribery:** when someone is offered money or a present so that they will do something, usually something that is not honest

The Victorian Era: The Golden Age of Poison

The 19th century is considered by many to be the golden age of poisonings. New advances in chemistry meant that many poisons became freely available to ordinary people for the first time. Substances like arsenic were commonly found in rat poison, cosmetics that women used, and cleaning products. Arsenic could be used secretly and provided very little in the way of evidence.

Importantly, the rise of life insurance proved too great a temptation for many, and became the main cause for the murder of husbands, wives, and even children, in an attempt to claim insurance money.

This was a period with many famous cases, including that of Belle Gunness, who placed personal ads in newspapers to find a husband, only to kill the men who came to visit her and steal their money. It is thought she killed as many as forty men, as well as two husbands and her own children.

The golden age of poisoning was not to last. Whereas scientific advances had previously been employed by criminals to commit crimes, by the beginning of the 20th century, chemistry was also being used by the police to catch criminals. Techniques were invented for detecting many common poisons, and police employed scientists to find evidence of poisoning. Gradually more and more poisoners were convicted, and the number of poisoning cases began to drop. The age of poisoners was over, and the new age of forensic science[5] had begun.

[5] **forensic science:** science used to help solve crimes

Forensic science is still used today to solve crimes.

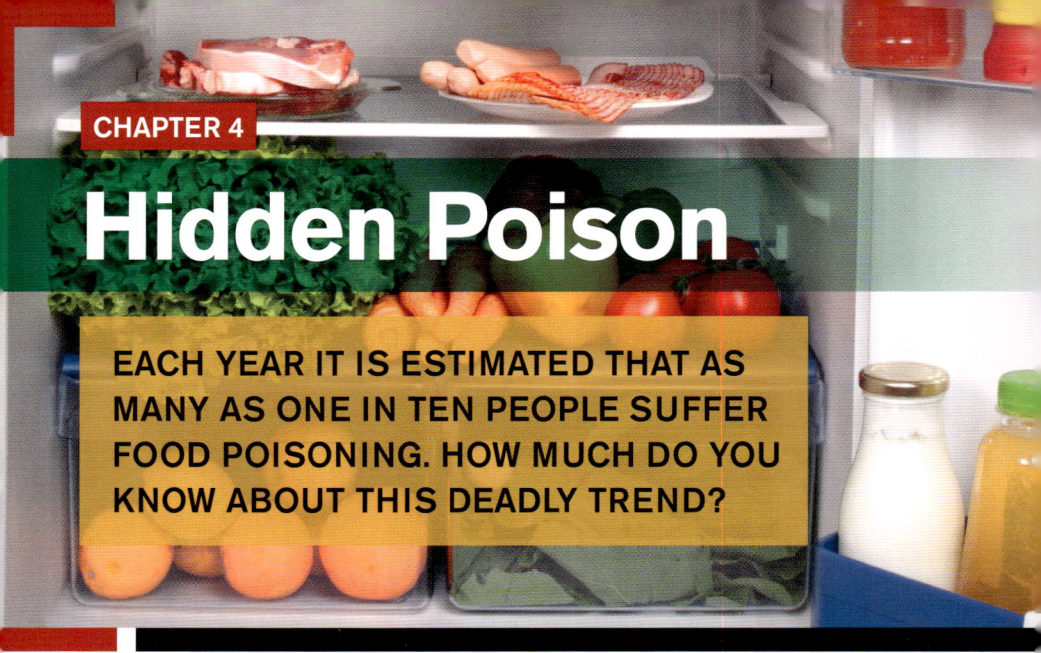

CHAPTER 4

Hidden Poison

EACH YEAR IT IS ESTIMATED THAT AS MANY AS ONE IN TEN PEOPLE SUFFER FOOD POISONING. HOW MUCH DO YOU KNOW ABOUT THIS DEADLY TREND?

1. Even if food looks and smells OK, it can be dangerous.

TRUE! It is difficult to spot the **germs** in food that can lead to food poisoning, as they do not usually affect the taste, look, or smell of the food you are eating.

2. The worst kinds of food poisoning are caused by germs.

TRUE! Some of the worst types of food poisoning are caused by *Escherichia coli* (commonly called *E. coli*) and *Salmonella*. Although these organisms are almost always found in our stomachs in small amounts, they are very dangerous at higher levels.

3. Keeping food in a refrigerator destroys poisonous bacteria.

FALSE! Bacteria grow best at temperatures between 5° and 63° Celsius. If it is any hotter, they are destroyed.

It is not as easy to destroy them with cold, however. Bacteria reproduce much more slowly below 5°C, and some are destroyed at low temperatures, but most of them can start to grow again as soon as the temperature rises. Even freezing will not protect foods forever.

4. Food should not be left sitting out, as bacteria increase very quickly.

TRUE! With the right temperature conditions, bacteria can reproduce as much as 500,000 times per hour! That's why an outbreak[6] of food poisoning can spread so fast.

5. If you wash your hands before cooking, food can't become infected.[7]

FALSE! Food can be infected not only by hands but also by things like dirty knives, towels, and kitchen surfaces. Everything should be well cleaned before cooking, and hands and knives should be washed often during cooking.

[6]**outbreak:** time when something suddenly begins, like a disease
[7]**infected:** containing harmful bacteria or viruses

Video Quest

Food poisoning

Watch this video to learn about food poisoning and the Centers for Disease Control (CDC). Where is *E. coli* found? Where did this outbreak of food poisoning originate?

CHAPTER 5

The Attraction of Poison

MYSTERY WRITER AGATHA CHRISTIE ONCE SAID, "GIVE ME A DECENT BOTTLE OF POISON, AND I'LL CONSTRUCT THE PERFECT CRIME."

More than half of Agatha Christie's famous whodunits (murder mystery stories, from the question "Who (has) 'done' it?") involve death by poison. Her personal favorite was the deadly arsenic – perhaps not surprising since she was born in 1890, when arsenic was the number one choice for any self-respecting murderer.

Poison has fascinated[8] people since the beginning of history. Plant and animal substances have been used both for celebrations and religious ceremonies. The same plant was sometimes used to achieve religious visions or, in a larger amount, to kill.

[8]**fascinate:** interest someone a lot

The secret knowledge of poisons, originally only available to priests and magicians, brought both a promise of power and fear of its consequences. There are many **myths** of forbidden secret knowledge.

In the Bible the very first story in the Old Testament tells us about the fruit of the Tree of Knowledge in the Garden of Eden, whose price is a loss of innocence and the promise of death. In modern texts, this fruit has been associated with the apple, which does actually have poisonous seeds.

The Greeks had many myths about poison. The story of Achilles, the Greek hero of the Trojan War, describes how his mother, Thetis, bathed him in the River Styx[9] to protect him from any weapon. However, so the story goes, she held on to him by his heel which was the only part not covered by the magic waters. Of course, Achilles is later killed by a poisoned arrow which hits him in that very place.

Achilles, famously killed by a poisoned arrow

[9]**River Styx:** in Ancient Greek stories, the connection between the world of the living and the world of the dead

Video Quest

The Rainbow Serpent

Watch this video about a famous cave painting of a snake to learn about the myth of the Rainbow Serpent. Who tells the stories? What is this snake associated with?

Snow White, poisoned by an apple

Medieval Europe has given us many stories involving poisons, often mixed by cruel, jealous witches. The idea of poisoned fruit, for example, appears in the fairy tale[10] of Snow White and the Seven Dwarves. An evil witch, jealous of Snow White's youth and beauty, gives her a poisoned apple that puts her into a deep sleep.

Shakespeare's plays are full of drugs, poisons, and love potions. Most famously, poison is the heartbreaking end chosen by Romeo when he believes his love Juliet to be dead.

In the 19th century, Alexandre Dumas often used poison to great effect, even as comedy. His novels are full of mystery, scandal,[11] and poison, from Catherine de Medici, in his novel *Queen Margot*, to the murder of the faithful Constance, D'Artagnan's lover in *The Three Musketeers*.

[10] **fairy tale:** a traditional story written for children, usually involving imaginary creatures and magic

[11] **scandal:** an event or action that causes the public to react with shock or anger

Poisons have continued to fascinate authors and readers in modern times. In Umberto Eco's *The Name of the Rose*, poison is used by a crazy, old, blind priest to prevent anyone reading a lost book on laughter, supposedly by the philosopher Aristotle. The murderer cannot tolerate the idea of destroying the book, however, so he sticks its pages together with a rare poison. As a reader licks his fingers to turn the sticky pages, he also poisons himself and dies horribly without finishing the book. Finally, the old priest eats the book, destroying it forever and taking his own life.

The relationship of forbidden knowledge, poison, and power is all too clear. It seems that poison continues to reflect our fascination, excitement, and fear of the natural world. And of what our knowledge of nature can lead us to do.

Romeo and Juliet

?

ANALYZE

Read Chapter 5, "The Attraction of Poison" again. Choose a story from the text that has an unexpected ending. Why is it unexpected?

CHAPTER 6

Whodunit?

THE LIVING ROOM AT CHESHAM HALL LOOKED OUT OVER THE ROOFTOPS OF THE NEARBY VILLAGE. IT WAS A WARM, LAZY AUGUST DAY. INSPECTOR GRANGER SIGHED AND TURNED AWAY FROM THE WINDOW.

He looked at the six anxious faces staring back at him. There was no doubt about it; one of them was a murderer. One of these fine, respectable figures had coldly slipped poison into the late-night drink of Chesham Hall's owner, the famous Egyptologist, Colonel Shelby-Sinclair.

Granger looked at the suspects one by one. Sitting calmly in an armchair was Eric Fortescue, the Colonel's banker, just up from London the night before bringing "important news."

On the sofa, the Colonel's secretary, Jemima, was crying softly.

To her right sat James Pickering, the Colonel's publisher, with his wife, Rose. They had also arrived the night before, "to talk business." The Inspector noticed that they never looked at each other, and their hands never touched.

Behind the sofa, shaken and nervous, stood Hugh Shelby, the Colonel's nephew and only heir.[12]

Finally, there was Asim, the Colonel's old Egyptian servant. Did he have something to hide?

Granger had to admit the idea had been brilliant. The poison's peachy taste would never have been noticed by the Colonel, who always drank homemade fruit tea before bed. His death would most certainly have been blamed on his own, badly made drink, had it not been for the fact that afterwards somebody had stabbed[13] *his already dead body as it lay cold in his bed.*

The Inspector cleared his throat. "Ladies and Gentlemen, it seems clear to me that the Colonel was MURDERED TWICE …"

Who do you think murdered Colonel Shelby-Sinclair? How did the person, or persons, do it? What might have been the motive(s)?

[12]**heir:** a person who has or is about to receive an inheritance

[13]**stab:** injure someone using a sharp, pointed object

APPLY

Finish the story of the murder of Colonel Shelby-Sinclair. What happens next?

After You Read

Read the following sentences and choose Ⓐ, Ⓑ, Ⓒ, or Ⓓ.

1 What did people think the young Mary Ann Cotton was like?

Ⓐ quiet
Ⓑ violent
Ⓒ friendly
Ⓓ passionate

2 Why could Mary easily commit her crimes?

Ⓐ Nobody knew her.
Ⓑ Poison was easy to get.
Ⓒ She had a lot of money.
Ⓓ She had many children.

3 Why is it hard to describe what a poison is?

Ⓐ They all have long Latin or Greek names.
Ⓑ They are always a mix of many chemicals.
Ⓒ All substances can be poisonous.
Ⓓ All poisons are medicines.

4 What is unusual about snake venom?

Ⓐ It is not poisonous to people.
Ⓑ It always kills slowly.
Ⓒ It is also used as a cure.
Ⓓ It smells very strong.

5 Why did people originally use poison?

Ⓐ to clean drinking water
Ⓑ to attract a partner
Ⓒ to kill animals and enemies
Ⓓ to cure snake and insect bites

6 Why are there fewer poisonings nowadays?

(A) Insurance companies pay less.

(B) Poisons are less dangerous.

(C) Punishment is much harder.

(D) Poisoning is harder to hide.

7 When do bacteria grow best?

(A) when the temperature is just right

(B) when you cook them

(C) when they are on dirty kitchen surfaces

(D) when they are in the human body

8 Which writer used poison in a funny way?

(A) Eco

(B) Christie

(C) Dumas

(D) Shakespeare

Complete the Chart

Poison has had many uses. Select two positive uses and two negative uses. Fill in the chart and then use your notes to summarize how poison has been used over time.

Positive	What poison?	How used?
Negative	What poison?	How used?

Answer Key

Words to Know, page 4
1 Bacteria **2** witch **3** weapons **4** fungus **5** potion

Words to Know, page 5
1 inheritance **2** insurance **3** arsenic **4** prey
5 antidotes **6** victim **7** motives

Predict, page 5 *Answers will vary.*

Evaluate, page 7 *Answers will vary.*

Video Quest, page 11
The southern Mexican states. They are milked in order to make an antidote from their venom.

Understand, page 13
The Latin word for poison comes from the name of the goddess of love in Roman mythology. The first poisons were used as love potions.

Video Quest, page 19
Normally in food but also in water. In cookie dough, probably in the wheat that was used to make the dough.

Video Quest, page 21
Aboriginal groups in Australia. It is associated with rain, rainbows, the rivers, and waterfalls.

Analyze, page 23 *Answers will vary.*

Apply, page 25 *Answers will vary.*

Choose the Correct Answers, page 26
1 C **2** B **3** C **4** C **5** C **6** D **7** A **8** C

Complete the Chart, page 27
Answers will vary.